Maggie's
Recipes

Keep It Simple

Maggie Corbett

Published by Campden Cookery
Manse Cottage, Chipping Campden, Gloucestershire, GL55 6AU

Artwork by Maggie Corbett

Layout and design by loosechippings.org

A big thank you to Arthur and Rachel Cunynghame for all their hard work in the preparation of this book.

Printed in England by J F Print Limited, Sparkford

ISBN 978-0-9567290-0-2

Contents

Although some of these recipes are clearly intended for specific situations, many can be adapted to varying uses: canapés, starters, light meals, dinner parties etc.

Grouping them in any meaningful way is therefore difficult.

The following gives an indication of where to find particular recipes, but I do recommend that you use the index at the back and approach the recipes with an open mind as to their uses.

Asparagus

& Prosciutto Rolls

method

Cook the asparagus in boiling water until just tender. Drain well and pat dry.

Brush the asparagus with the melted butter, then roll in the Parmesan.

Wrap each spear in the ham.

Place on a baking tray lined with non-stick baking paper. Sprinkle the nutmeg, some ground black pepper and any remaining Parmesan over the top.

Bake in a hot oven for about 5 minutes. Remove from the oven. Pour a little lemon juice over the top.

Serve.

ingredients
makes 12 pieces

6 Slices of Prosciutto, cut in half.

12 Asparagus spears, about 7cm/3" long.

50g/2oz Melted butter.

25g/1oz Grated Parmesan.

Juice of half a lemon.

Freshly grated nutmeg.

Smoked Salmon
& Dill Pinwheels

method

Chop the dill and mix with softened butter.

Cut the crusts off the brown bread and roll out between two sheets of cling film until very thin.

Spread with dill butter.

Place smoked salmon on bread leaving 1cm/½" gap at top.

Roll up. Chill for 1 hour. Slice into pinwheels. Can be frozen before slicing.

ingredients
each pin wheel makes 6 pieces

50g/2oz Butter.

15g/½oz Dill.

225g/8oz Smoked salmon.

6 Slices of medium cut sliced brown bread.

Taramasalta

TIP
Do not use olive oil that is too strong,
otherwise it will overpower the final
result. I use a Greek olive oil, but am
not allowed to mention the name,
sorry!

TIP
To make breadcrumbs, use a sliced
loaf, preferably out of date. Take off
the crusts, which can be cut into cubes
and frozen for later use as croutons.
Then whizz the bread in a food
processor and again freeze for use as
wanted.

ingredients
serves 8

325g/12oz Smoked cod's roe.

100ml/¼pt Olive oil.

2 Lemons, juiced.

225g/8oz breadcrumbs.

225ml/½pt Double cream.

Black pepper.

method

Skin the cod's roe and place in a food processor with oil, lemon juice and pepper and whizz until smooth.

Add the breadcrumbs and whizz again.

Add the cream.

Serve with bread and olives.

7

Warm Asparagus Rolls

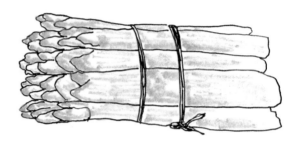

method

Cook the asparagus in boiling water until cooked. Run under cold water and cool.

Take the crusts off the bread and roll out between two sheets of cling film until thin.

Spread the cream cheese over the bread and grind pepper over the top.

ingredients

makes 6 pieces

1 Large slice of white bread.

1 Spear fresh Asparagus.

Full fat cream cheese.

Melted butter.

Place the asparagus on the edge of the bread and roll up like a Swiss roll.

Brush with melted butter and bake in a hot oven at 180c/350f for 5-8 minutes until golden brown.

Cool slightly and cut up into small rolls with a sharp knife and serve

Pistachio
& Chilli Biscuits

TIP
When glazing anything, always use egg yolk rather than a whole egg. You will get a much better finish and it will look more professional.

ingredients
makes approx 48 pieces

110g/4oz Plain flour.

½tsp Dried mustard powder.

75g/3oz Butter, diced.

½tsp Mild chilli powder.

50g/2oz Tasty Cheddar cheese, grated.

25g/1oz Fresh Parmesan, grated.

50g/2oz Pistachio nuts, shelled and roughly chopped.

2 Egg yolks to glaze.

method

Place all the ingredients, apart from the egg yolks, in a food processor, and whizz until the mixture comes together. Turn out onto a floured surface.

Roll out the mixture, cut out with fancy cutters, place on a baking tray which has been covered with non-stick baking paper. Glaze with the egg yolk.

Bake at 160c/325f for about 10 minutes until golden.

Cool and store in an airtight container.

9

Melba Toast

method

Place 2 slices of bread under a pre-heated hot grill. Toast both sides.

Remove the crusts, slice through the middle with a sharp knife, placing your hand on top of the toast as you do this. You should now have 4 slices.

Toast the uncooked sides; they should curl up with the heat. Be very careful at this stage as it can burn very easily.

ingredients
makes 16 slices

Repeat with the rest of the bread.

8 Slices of wholemeal or white medium sliced bread.

When cool, store in an airtight container, lined with baking paper, for up to 1 week.

Chicken Liver
& Pistachio Pâté

ingredients
serves 8-10

4 Rashers thin, streaky, smoked bacon.

700g/1½lb Chicken livers.

2 Cloves garlic, crushed.

1 Pinch of allspice.

125g/4oz Chestnut mushrooms, chopped.

2 Onions, chopped .

200g/7oz Light cream cheese.

30ml/2tbsp Double cream.

60g/2oz Pistachio nuts, roughly chopped.

1 tbsp Parsley, chopped.

1 tbsp Chives, chopped.

1 tbsp Thyme, chopped.

155g/5oz Butter.

method

Clean the chicken livers (Tip p.90)

Fry the bacon in a pan until brown. Remove with a slotted spoon.

Add 50g/2oz of the butter to the pan and melt. Add the livers, fry over a high heat until browned all over but pink inside. Remove from the pan.

Add the onions, garlic and mushrooms to the pan, and fry until soft.

Mix the livers, bacon, onions, garlic, cream cheese, herbs, allspice, cream, pistachio nuts and residue from the pan together.

Transfer to a blender or food processor and blend until smooth. Season.

Spoon the pâté into pots and top with the remaining butter which has been melted and clarified (Tip p.46). Chill.

Spinach Pâté

SPINACH

ingredients
serves 6-8 portions

1kg/2lb Spinach.

50g/2oz tin Anchovies, oil removed.

3 Eggs, hard boiled, peeled and quartered.

100g/4oz Butter, melted.

1tbsp Double cream.

1tsp Basil, chopped.

1 level tsp Ready-made English mustard.

¼tsp Tabasco sauce.

Salt and pepper.

method

Wash the spinach and cook until wilted. Squeeze dry.

Put all the ingredients into a food processor and blend until smooth.

Place in a serving dish and chill.

Serve with Melba toast. (See p. 10)

Chicken, Lemon & Pistachio Terrine

LEMON

method

ingredients
serves 8-10 as a starter

1 Shallot, chopped.

12g/1½oz Butter.

2 Chicken breasts, diced.

2 Eggs, beaten.

1 Lemon, zest.

4tbsp Double cream.

25g/1oz Fresh white breadcrumbs. (Tip p.7)

50g/2oz Pistachio nuts, shelled.

2tsp Thyme, chopped.

8 Rashers thin, streaky, smoked bacon.

Melt the butter in a pan and add the shallot. Cook until softened but not coloured.

Mix together all the ingredients, except the bacon, in a mixing bowl. Add salt and pepper.

Line a 450g/1lb loaf tin with the bacon.

Add the chicken mixture to the tin. Place in a water bath. (Tip p.83)

Cook for approx 1 hour until the top is firm and the juices run clear.

Cover the terrine with non-stick baking paper and weight the top.

Cool. Place in the refrigerator overnight, with the weights still on top.

Turn out. Serve.

The terrine can be frozen at this stage.

Cheese Pastry

ingredients

makes about 400g/14oz pastry

225g/8oz Plain flour.

50g/2oz Butter, diced.

50g/2oz Trex.

25g/1oz Parmesan cheese, grated.

50g/2oz Cheddar cheese, grated.

½tsp English mustard powder.

method

Place all the ingredients in a food processor with a plastic blade. Process until the mixture resembles fine breadcrumbs.

Add 4tbsp cold water. Process again until the mixture comes together.

Wrap in cling film. Chill in the refrigerator for at least 30 minutes. The pastry may be frozen.

Feta & Mint

Pastries

NUTMEG

ingredients
makes approx 48 pastries

method

400g/14oz Cheese pastry.
(See p. 14)

Roll out the pastry and line some mini,
greased flan cases.

200g/7oz Feta cheese,
drained and crumbled.

Bake blind until the pastry is golden brown.
(Tip p.87)

1 Egg yolk.

Mix the rest of the ingredients together.

A Pinch of nutmeg and
black pepper.

Place the filling into the cases.

Place on a baking tray and cook in a hot
oven at 160c/325f for about 7 minutes.

1tbsp Chopped chives.

1tbsp Chopped mint.

Serve.

Mini Flans

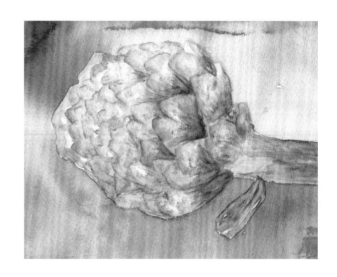

ingredients
makes about 60 mini flans

800g/28oz Cheese pastry.
(twice the quantity on p. 14)

275ml/½pt Double cream.

4 Eggs, beaten.

25ml/1floz Milk.

75g/3oz Grated Cheddar
cheese.

25g/1oz Grated Parmesan
cheese.

1 Small onion, finely
chopped, softened not
browned in butter in a pan.

4 Artichoke hearts, chopped.

8 Rashers of streaky, smoked
Bacon, cut into lardons, dry
fried until crisp.

method

Mix cream, eggs, milk and pepper together.

Roll out the pastry and cut out. Place in greased flan cases.

Add a little filling, followed by a pinch of Parmesan and Cheddar. Fill with egg mixture.

Bake at 180c/350f for about 12-15 minutes until golden.

Turn out onto a cooling wire. When cold you can freeze in a plastic container. Heat from frozen in a hot oven.

Pesto

OLIVIO IN CHIANTI.
M Corbett.

ingredients
makes one jar

50g/2oz Rocket or basil.

1tbsp Olive oil.

1tbsp Pine nuts.

1 Clove garlic, peeled and crushed.

1tbsp Fresh Parmesan, grated.

TIP
Pesto can be frozen in small containers. Defrost overnight in the refrigerator before use.

method

Whizz all ingredients together.

Keep in a screw top jar in the refrigerator.

Italian Toasties

ingredients
makes about 5 slices

1 Loaf Focaccia or Ciabatta bread, cut into roughly 10cm/4" squares.

250g/8oz Mozzarella cheese, torn into small pieces.

250g/8oz Sun-dried tomatoes.

8tsp Homemade pesto. (See p.17)

2tbsp Basil, roughly chopped.

method

Lightly toast the bread on both sides.

Spread each slice with pesto, then a little Mozzarella, followed by the tomatoes and then more Mozzarella.

Season.

Grill 3-4 minutes until the cheese has melted.

Sprinkle with basil, serve.

Spicy Avocado Dip

ingredients

serves 6-8

2 Large or 4 small Avocados, peeled and stoned.

200g/8oz Low fat cream cheese.

Juice of 2 Limes.

½tsp Lemon grass paste.

½tsp Coriander paste.

½tsp Chilli paste.

2 Cloves of Garlic, peeled and crushed.

Salt and Pepper.

TIP
All the pastes mentioned can be found in the cooler section with the salads in any supermarket. Once opened keep in the refrigerator.

method

Place all ingredients in a food processor and whizz until smooth.

Serve with crudités, crisps or tortilla chips.

Sun-dried Tomato, Cheese & Basil Palmiers

method

Roll out the pastry to 15cmx35cm/6"x14" and trim the edges.

Spread the cheese, sun-dried tomatoes and basil evenly over the pastry.

Roll up the ends tightly to meet in the middle. Wet the edges to get a good seal.

Cover with cling film and chill for 30 minutes, or until firm.

Brush with beaten egg, cut into 1cm/½" slices.

ingredients
makes about 12 palmiers

225g/8oz Puff pastry.

50g/2oz Cheddar cheese, grated.

2tbsp Sun-dried tomatoes, chopped.

1tbsp Fresh Basil, chopped.

Place on a baking tray lined with non-stick baking paper.

Bake at 180c/350f for approx 10 minutes or until golden brown.

To freeze, cool first.

Place in an airtight plastic container.

To reheat from frozen, cook in a hot oven at 180c/350f until crisp.

Mini Bangers & Mustard Mash

TIP
Always use the tin foil non-shiny side
next to the food you are covering.
Certain foods react to the foil.
eg. Bacon.

method

Place the potatoes in cold water and add salt. Bring to the boil and cook for approx 20 minutes until soft. Drain.

ingredients
makes 20 sausages

Mash. Add the butter, mustard and egg yolk. Mix well.

20 Cooked cocktail sausages.

Heat the sausages in a hot oven at 180c/350f for 5 minutes. Remove and make a slice across the top, making sure not to cut through to the bottom.

2 Medium potatoes, peeled and halved.

Place the potato in a piping bag and pipe down the middle of the cut sausage.

1 Egg yolk.

13g/½oz Butter.

To reheat loosely cover with foil. Place in a pre-heated oven at 160c/325f for 15 minutes.

1tsp Grainy mustard.

21

Baked Spinach Gnocchi

with Fresh Tomato Sauce

ingredients
serves 6

175g/6oz Spinach,
squeezed dry, roughly
chopped and cooked.

110g/4oz Ricotta cheese.

25g/1oz Parmesan cheese,
freshly grated.

1 Egg, beaten.

3dtsp Plain flour.

12g/½oz Butter, softened.

1 pinch Grated nutmeg.

To serve

50g/2oz Butter, melted.

3tbsp Fresh Parmesan,
grated.

Fresh tomato sauce (See
p.23)

method

Place all the ingredients in a food processor
with salt and pepper. Whizz until well
combined. Turn into a bowl. Chill in the
refrigerator for at least 30 minutes.

Take tsps of the mixture and shape into
small lozenges.

Bring a large pan of salted water to boil.
Drop in the gnocchi mixture, cook for
about 3-4 minutes until they rise to the
surface. Drain well on kitchen paper.

Place in a gratin dish, pour a little melted
butter over the top and sprinkle with
Parmesan. Bake in a hot oven at 160c/325f
for 10 minutes.

Serve with the tomato sauce.

Fresh Tomato Sauce

ingredients
makes enough for about 6

4 Large Vine tomatoes, peeled, seeded and chopped. (Tip p.32)

1 Clove of garlic, peeled and crushed.

1tsp Thyme, chopped.

1tbsn Basil, roughly chopped.

1 Banana shallot, peeled and chopped.

1 Stick of celery, chopped.

1tbsn Olive oil.

1tsp Brown sugar.

Salt and Pepper.

method

Place the oil in a pan, add the shallot, celery and garlic.

Cook until soft, but not coloured.

Add the tomatoes, thyme, basil, sugar, salt and pepper.

Cook on a low heat for 15 minutes.

Spaghetti

with Clams, Garlic & Chilli

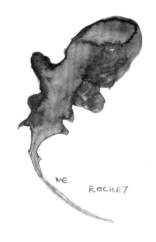

ROCKET

ingredients
serves 4

225g/8oz Spaghetti.

3 Cloves garlic, peeled and sliced.

2 Red chillies, seeded and chopped.

1 Red onion, peeled and chopped finely.

280g/10oz Tin of baby clams, drained.

125ml/4½floz Olive oil.

1 Lemon, juice of.

2tbsp Flat leaf parsley, chopped.

50g/2oz Rocket.

50g/2oz Parmesan cheese, freshly grated.

method

Pour the olive oil into a pan.

Add the onions, garlic and chilli. Cook over a low heat until soft but not coloured.

Add the lemon juice and rocket and wilt.

Add the clams and heat through gently.

Cook the spaghetti in boiling salted water until al dente. Drain.

Add the spaghetti to the sauce, season and toss until well coated.

Serve sprinkled with parsley & Parmesan.

Spicy Tagliatelle

with Garlic, Tomato & Mushrooms

ingredients
serves 6-8

1 pinch of Brown sugar.

1tbsp Olive oil.

250g/9oz Chestnut mushrooms, wiped with kitchen roll and sliced.

2 Cloves garlic, peeled and crushed.

1 Onion, peeled and chopped.

3 Sticks of celery, washed and chopped.

400g/14oz Tin chopped tomatoes.

1 Red Chilli, seeded and sliced.

2tsp Fresh thyme, chopped.

1tbsp Fresh parsley, chopped.

325g/12oz Tagliatelle.

method

Place the oil in a pan, add the onions, garlic and celery. Cook until soft.

Add the mushrooms and increase the heat. Cook for 3-4 minutes until golden.

Reduce the heat and add the chilli, tomatoes and thyme. Cook for 20 minutes.

Add a pinch of brown sugar.

Cook the tagliatelle in boiling salted water until al dente. Drain.

Toss the tagliatelle through the sauce. Add the chopped parsley. Serve.

Goats Cheese Salad

with Walnuts & Warm Dressing

TIP
Salad leaves can be washed the day before you want to use them. Wash well in cold water, spin in a salad spinner to remove the excess water (or place in a clean tea towel, bring the corners together and shake vigorously). Place the lettuce in a zip lock bag and refrigerate until needed.

ingredients
serves 6

1 Bag Mixed salad leaves, washed and drained.

110g/4oz Walnut bits.

6 Slices of Chèvre, with rind on (or use a small goats cheese cut in half).

6tbsp Sunflower oil.

2tbsp White wine vinegar.

1tsp Caster sugar.

1tsp Dijon mustard.

Salt and pepper.

method

Fry the walnuts in the sunflower oil until crisp. Drain and keep warm.

Mix the oil in which you have cooked the walnuts with the vinegar, mustard, sugar, salt and pepper. Whisk and keep warm.

Place the goats cheese on a baking sheet covered with non-stick baking paper and cook at top of the oven at 200c/400f for approx 10 minutes until the cheese is runny.

Place on mixed leaves and sprinkle with walnuts.

Drizzle dressing over the top and serve.

Beetroot, Apple & Gorsehill Abbey Brie Salad

ingredients
serves 6

1 Bag mixed leaves, washed and drained.

1 Bunch Beetroot, washed and stalks removed.

4 Local Eating apples.

50g/2oz Walnuts.

Juice of 1 Lemon.

1 Whole Gorsehill Abbey Brie. (or any small Brie or Camembert cheese)

1tbsp Olive oil.

Dressing

50ml/2floz Olive oil.

25ml/1floz Lemon juice.

1tsp Caster sugar.

1tsp Dijon mustard.

1tbsp Dill, chopped.

Salt and Pepper.

method

Wrap the beetroot individually in tin foil. Place on a baking tray and bake for 1hour at 160c/325f. Remove from the oven. Cool. Peel and slice.

Place the Brie in an ovenproof dish and bake at 160c/325f for 15-20 minutes until hot.

Peel and core the apples, and place in a bowl with the lemon juice and a little water.

Fry the walnuts in the oil until crisp. Drain. Keep warm.

Place the mixed leaves in a salad bowl. Add the beetroot and the apple (which has been well drained). Followed by spoonfuls of hot Brie and then the walnuts.

Dressing

Place all ingredients for the dressing in a jam jar, screw on the lid and shake well.

Drizzle the dressing over the top of the salad. Serve.

Mango, Parma Ham & Ricotta Salad

ingredients

serves 8

175g/6oz Ricotta cheese.

2tbsp Mixed herbs, chopped
(chives, basil, flat leaf parsley
and tarragon).

½tsp Lemon juice.

Salt and pepper.

1 Fresh, ripe mango, sliced.

110g/4oz Parma ham.

50g/2oz Watercress leaves.

50g/2oz Black olives, pitted.

Lemon rind shredded and
blanched to garnish.

WATERCRESS

Dressing

1 Ripe tomato, skinned,
seeded and diced. (Tip p.32)

1 Small shallot, finely
chopped.

1 Clove garlic, crushed.

1tsp Grated lemon rind.

1tsp Lemon juice.

½tsp White wine vinegar.

4tbsp Olive oil.

method

Beat the Ricotta with the herbs, lemon juice
and salt and pepper. Cover and chill for 30
minutes.

To make the dressing, put all the ingredients
into a screw top jar and shake well. Season.

Divide the mango between serving plates
and top with Parma ham, watercress leaves
and olives. Form the Ricotta mixture
into small quenelle shapes between two
teaspoons and place on top of salad.

Spoon the dressing over the salad and
garnish with lemon shreds.

Scallop & Bacon Salad

with Crispy Sage Leaves

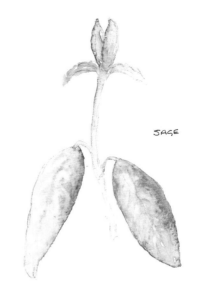

SAGE

ingredients
serves 4-6

12 Scallops, sliced in half horizontally.

12 Slices streaky smoked bacon, diced.

25g/1oz Butter.

Sage leaves.

1 Bag Mixed leaves. (Tip p.26)

150ml/5floz Sunflower oil.

Lime Dressing
(place all ingredients below in a jar and shake)

6tbsp Oil.

1tbsp Vinegar.

2 Limes, grated and juiced.

1tsp Dijon mustard.

2tsp Sugar.

method

Melt half the butter in a frying pan and add the bacon. Cook until crisp. Drain and keep warm.

Fry the sage leaves in the sunflower oil until crisp. Drain on kitchen paper and keep warm.

Heat the rest of the butter in the frying pan and add the scallops and ground pepper. Fry on both sides for 2 minutes each.

Place the scallops on the dressed leaves and sprinkle the bacon over the top, followed by the sage leaves.

Warm Partridge Salad

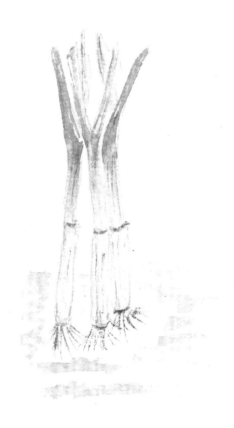

ingredients
serves 6

50g/2oz Butter.

100g/4oz Streaky bacon, diced.

100g/4oz Chestnut or button mushrooms, sliced.

200g/8oz Cooked partridge breast, cut into thin strips.

3 Spring onions cut into 1cm/½" strips.

1 Bag Mixed salad leaves, washed and drained. (Tip p.26)

Dressing

4tbsp Olive oil.

1tbsp Balsamic vinegar.

Pinch golden caster sugar.

1 Clove garlic, crushed.

1tbsp Parsley, chopped.

Salt and pepper.

method

Mix all the dressing ingredients together.

Melt the butter in a frying pan and add the bacon. Cook until golden and add the mushrooms. Fry for 2 minutes. Add the spring onions and partridge and cook until warmed through.

Serve on a bed of leaves with the dressing drizzled over the top.

Rocket Roulade with Smoked Salmon, Dill & Pickled Ginger

ingredients

serves 8

100g/4oz Rocket.

1tbsp Fromage frais.

4 Eggs, separated.

175g/6oz Light cream cheese.

12g/½oz Butter, softened.

225g/8oz Smoked salmon.

1tbsp Chopped dill.

25g/1oz Pickled ginger, chopped.

25g/1oz Grated fresh Parmesan.

method

Put the rocket in a food processor with the fromage frais, butter, salt and pepper, and blitz.

Add the egg yolks, one by one.

Place the mixture in a bowl. Whisk the egg whites until stiff but not dry, fold into the rocket mixture.

Pour into a baking tray, lined with non-stick baking paper. Bake at 160c/325f for about 15 minutes until the top is firm. Take out of the oven, cover with a clean tea towel and cool slightly.

Turn out onto another piece of parchment, sprinkled with the Parmesan cheese. Trim the edges.

Mix the cream cheese, dill, salt and pepper together. Spread over the roulade.

Sprinkle the smoked salmon and pickled ginger over the top. Roll up the roulade. Chill until needed.

Slice and serve. This will freeze.

Tomato, Cheese & Dijon Flan

with a Herb & Garlic Topping

ROSEMARY

TIP
To skin tomatoes, make a small cut in the top of the tomato, where the stem is attached. Drop into a pan of boiling water for 10 seconds. Remove with a slotted spoon and place in cold water. The skin should peel off very easily, if not put back into the boiling water for another second or two.

ingredients
serves 6

170g/6½oz All butter puff pastry.

450g/1lb Vine tomatoes.

110g/4oz Grated cheddar cheese.

1tsp Chopped fresh thyme.

2tsp Chopped fresh rosemary.

2tbsp Dijon mustard.

55g/2oz Fresh white breadcrumbs. (Tip p.7)

2tbsp Olive oil.

1 Clove garlic crushed.

Salt and pepper.

method

Roll out the pastry and line a 20cm/8" flan case. Chill for 10 minutes. Bake blind at 160c/325f until the pastry is golden.

Place the oil in a frying pan, add the garlic and cook until soft but not coloured. Add the thyme, rosemary and breadcrumbs. Stir until pale golden.

Spread the mustard over the flan case base. Slice the tomatoes, place over the mustard, add salt and pepper.

Sprinkle the cheese over the tomatoes, followed by the crumbs.

Bake for approximately 30 minutes until the crumbs are golden brown.

Macaroni

with a difference

ingredients
serves 4

1ltr/2pt Vegetable stock.

325g/12oz Macaroni.

325g/12oz New Potatoes, peeled and cubed.

1 Medium onion, peeled and chopped.

25g/1oz Butter.

1 Red chilli, seeded and chopped.

1tsp Thyme, chopped.

1 Clove garlic, peeled and crushed.

50g/2oz Rocket, chopped.

110g/4oz Spinach, washed and chopped.

1tbsp Parsley, chopped.

50g/2oz Fresh Parmesan, grated.

SPINACH

method

Melt the butter in a large saucepan, add the onion, garlic and chilli. Soften.

Add the thyme, macaroni, potatoes and stock. Bring to the boil. Simmer until the potatoes and macaroni are soft.

Add the rocket and spinach. Wilt.

Serve with grated Parmesan and chopped parsley over the top.

Pasta with Smoked Haddock
& Wilted Spinach

SPINACH

ingredients
serves 4

225g/8oz Tagliatelle.

450g/1lb Undyed Smoked
Haddock, skinned.

15g/½oz Butter.

450g/1lb Baby spinach,
washed.

150ml/5floz Soured cream.

2tbsp Fresh chives,
snipped.

1tbsp Lemon juice.

Pinch nutmeg.

Salt and pepper.

method

Place the pasta in boiling salted water and
cook for approx 7 minutes.

Slice the haddock into 3cm/1½" diagonal
pieces.

Melt the butter in a frying pan, add the fish.
Cook for 4-5 minutes.

Drain the pasta. Put the spinach in the pasta
pan and wilt for approx 2-3 minutes.

Return the pasta to the pan, add the soured
cream, lemon juice, nutmeg, chives, salt and
pepper, and heat.

Add the fish and serve.

Potato & Parsnip Gratinée

ingredients
serves 8

700g/1½lb Potatoes, peeled.

700g/1½lb Parsnips, peeled and hard cores removed. (Tip p.38)

1 Shallot, peeled and chopped.

25g/1oz butter.

1 Clove garlic, peeled and crushed.

425g/¾pt Single cream.

1tbsp Chives, snipped.

50g/2oz Cheddar cheese, grated.

Topping

3tbsp Fresh white breadcrumbs mixed (Tip p.7) with 25g/1oz grated Cheddar cheese.

method

Grate the potato and parsnips together, squeeze out the liquid and place in a large bowl.

Melt the butter in a pan and add the shallot and garlic. Soften.

Add this to the parsnip mixture with the cream, cheese, chives, salt and pepper. Mix well.

Spoon into a greased oven proof dish. Top with the breadcrumbs and cheese.

Bake approximately 1 hour at 160c/325f.

Roasted Mediterranean Vegetables

method

Slice the aubergine, salt and place in a colander. Leave for 15 minutes to remove the bitter juices. Wash, drain and pat dry with kitchen roll.

Place the peppers on a baking tray, place in a preheated oven at 180c/350f until the outsides are charred.

Remove from the oven, cover with a clean tea towel and leave to go cold. Skin, seed and slice.

Pour the oil into a casserole dish, add the onions and cook until soft.

Add the drained aubergines, courgettes, garlic and tomatoes. Add salt and pepper.

Place the lid on the casserole, place in the oven at 180c/350f for 15-20 minutes until just soft. Add the peppers and basil. Serve.

ingredients
serves 6-8

1 Small Aubergine.

2 Medium Courgettes, sliced.

1 Red onion, peeled, halved and sliced.

2 Cloves of Garlic, peeled and crushed.

2 Red peppers.

6 Vine tomatoes, skinned and seeded. (Tip p.32)

2tbsp Olive oil.

8 Basil leaves, torn into bits.

Cauliflower Polonaise

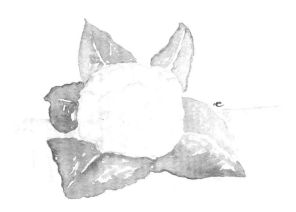

method

Place the eggs in boiling water and boil for 10 minutes.

Take off the heat and run the pan under cold water.

Remove the eggs and peel. Mash with a potato masher.

Place the cauliflower in a pan of boiling water and cook until just starting to soften. Add a pinch of salt. Boil for 1 minute and then drain.

While the cauliflower is cooking, melt the butter in a pan, add the breadcrumbs, and cook until golden brown.

Remove from the heat, add the herbs and chopped egg and combine.

Place the cauliflower in a dish and sprinkle with the breadcrumbs. Serve.

ingredients
serves 4

1 Small Cauliflower, outer leaves removed.

2 Eggs.

1oz Breadcrumbs. (Tip p.7)

1tbsp Parsley, chopped.

1tsp Chives, snipped.

25g/1oz Butter.

Parmesan Parsnips

TIP

If the parsnips are at the end of the season, about December, remove the hard core from the centre, as this will not soften when cooked.

ingredients
serves 6

500g/1lb Parsnips, peeled and cut into eighths.

50g/2oz Plain flour.

25g/1oz Parmesan, grated.

3tbsp Olive oil.

Salt and Pepper.

method

Place the parsnips in a pan of cold water with a pinch of salt. Bring to the boil. Simmer until just tender. Drain.

Mix the cheese, flour, salt and pepper together in a bowl, add the drained parsnips and toss to coat.

Heat the oil in a roasting pan, add the parsnips and cook until golden brown, approximately 45mins at 180c/350f.

Carrots with Cumin

ingredients
serves 4

1tsp Cumin seeds, dry-pan fried to release the flavour.

1 Bunch Baby Carrots.

1tsp Demerara sugar.

25g/1oz Butter.

Pinch of salt.

method

Top and tail the carrots, wash and leave whole.

Place the carrots in a pan of cold water with the sugar and salt.

Bring to the boil, simmer until al dente. Drain.

Melt the butter, add the cumin and carrots, toss and serve.

Brussel Sprouts with Almonds

ingredients
serves 6

500g/1lb Brussel sprouts.

50g/2oz Butter.

50g/2oz Flaked Almonds.

Pinch of salt.

method

Remove the outer leaves from the sprouts and make a small cross on the base (this helps the sprouts to cook quickly).

Place the sprouts in boiling water, bring back to the boil and cook until just tender. Add a pinch of salt and cook for 1 more minute. Drain.

While the sprouts are cooking, melt the butter in a pan, add the almonds and cook until brown, stirring all the time.

Place the sprouts in a warmed serving dish. Sprinkle the nuts and butter over the top. Serve.

Mild Curried Roasted Butternut Squash & Chestnut Soup

ingredients

serves 6

2 Butternut squash, halved and the seeds removed.

2tbsp Olive oil.

3 Onions, peeled and chopped.

2 Cloves of garlic, peeled and crushed.

2tsp Curry powder.

½ Whole nutmeg, grated.

1.375ltr/2½pt Vegetable stock.

250g/9oz Whole vacuum packed chestnuts, roughly chopped.

1 Large can of low fat coconut milk.

method

Place the squash on a baking tray, cut side up. Drizzle with half the oil and sprinkle with nutmeg. Bake in an oven at 160c/325f for 1 hour. Cool.

Place the remainder of the oil in a saucepan, add the onions and garlic. Cook until soft.

Add the curry powder and cook out for 2 minutes.

Add the stock and coconut milk and bring up to simmering point. Cook for 15 minutes.

Scoop out the flesh of the squash, add to the stock mixture. Bring back to the boil and simmer 5 minutes.

Liquidise.

Reheat the soup, add the chestnuts. Serve.

Roasted Red Pepper, Harrissa & Sweet Potato Soup

method

Roast the peppers on a baking tray in a hot oven, turning half way through, for about 20 minutes, until charred.

Remove from the oven, place a clean tea towel over the top and cool slightly.

Peel the peppers and remove the seeds. Slice.

Heat the oil in a saucepan, add the onions and garlic and soften but do not colour.

Add the harrissa paste, tomatoes, potatoes, stock and the sliced peppers.

Simmer until the potatoes are cooked.

Whizz in a blender. Serve.

ingredients
serves 8

325g/12oz Sweet potatoes, peeled and diced.

3 Large red peppers.

1tbsp Olive oil.

3 Cloves of garlic, peeled and crushed.

400g/14oz Tin chopped tomatoes.

1.75ltr/3pt Chicken stock made with 3 cubes.

2tsp Harrissa paste.

Stilton & Wine Soup

with Parmesan Crisps

ingredients
serves 6

50g/2oz Butter.

1 Medium onion, chopped.

2 Sticks celery, chopped.

40g/1½oz Flour.

3tbsp White wine.

850mls/1½pts Chicken stock made with 2 cubes.

275mls/½pt Semi skimmed milk.

110g/4oz Stilton cheese, crumbled.

110g/4oz Cheddar cheese, grated.

Parmesan Crisps

12tsp Parmesan.

method

Melt the butter and add the onion and celery. Soften but do not colour.

Add the flour and cook out for 2 minutes.

Add the wine and the stock and bring to simmering point. Simmer for 30 minutes. Remove from the heat.

Add both cheeses and stir until melted.

Add milk.

Purée in a liquidiser and adjust seasoning.

Reheat but do not allow to boil.

Parmesan Crisps

Place freshly grated Parmesan in small heaps (approx 1 large teaspoon each) on non-stick baking paper on a tray.

Place in a very hot oven at 180c/350f for approx 5 minutes until golden brown. Cool and serve separately.

Wild Mushroom & Game Soup

ingredients
serves 8

Game stock

1 Whole pheasant.

3 Sticks celery.

2.3ltr/4pt Cold water.

1 Large onion, peeled and quartered.

4 Parsley stalks.

1 Sprig thyme.

1 Bay leaf.

1 Carrot.

10 Peppercorns.

Salt.

Soup

1.7ltr/3pt Game stock (see above)

250g/9oz Diced, cooked pheasant meat.

500g/1lb Mixed wild mushrooms, chopped.

1tsp Thyme.

2 Medium onions, finely chopped.

25g/1oz Butter.

25g/1oz Flour.

Salt and pepper.

method

Game stock

Put all the ingredients in a large saucepan and bring to the boil (use the breasts for the soup).

Simmer for approx 1½ hours and then strain.

Soup

Melt the butter in a large pan and add the onion. Soften but do not colour. Add the mushrooms and cook for approx 5 minutes.

Add the flour and cook out.

Slowly add the stock and the thyme and bring to the boil. Simmer for ½ hour.

Add the meat and adjust the seasoning.

Prawn & Chilli Noodle Broth

ingredients
serves 8

100g/4oz French beans, cut into three.

100g/4oz Baby corn, sliced.

1 Red chilli, seeded and thinly sliced.

5cm/2" Fresh Root Ginger, peeled and grated.

4 Spring onions, chopped.

1.7ltr/3pt Chicken stock made with 3 cubes.

110g/4oz Dried thread egg noodles.

1 Lime, juiced.

6tbsp Light soy sauce.

2tbsp Dry sherry.

225g/8oz Peeled prawns. (Tip p.90)

2tbsp Fresh coriander, chopped.

method

Put the stock into a large pan and add the noodles, beans, corn, chilli and ginger. Bring to the boil and simmer for 10 minutes.

Add the soy sauce, sherry, lime juice and simmer for a further 4 minutes.

Add prawns and spring onions and heat through.

Serve in bowls and sprinkle with coriander.

Potted Prawns

TIP
To make clarified butter, melt butter in a pan, remove the foam on top with a spoon, pour off and keep the clear liquid, discarding the white residue at the bottom.

ingredients
serves 6

225g/8oz Prawns. (Tip p.90)

225g/8oz Unsalted butter.

1tsp Ground mace.

½tsp Mixed spice.

½tsp Ground black pepper.

½tsp Paprika pepper.

method

Clarify the butter.

Put the prawns into a frying pan and add enough clarified butter to moisten well.

Add the spices and cook over a high heat until the prawns are hot.

Turn into ramekins and press down.

Seal with remainder of the clarified butter. Chill.

Baked Cod

with Granny's Egg Sauce

ingredients

serves 6

3 Cod loins.

75g/3oz Breadcrumbs. (Tip p.7)

150g/6oz Butter, melted.

Sauce

2 Eggs.

1tbsp Coriander, chopped. (optional)

1tsp Curry powder.

25g/1oz Butter.

12g/½oz Plain flour.

225ml/8floz Milk.

1 Lemon, cut in to wedges.

Salt and Pepper.

method

Place fish on a baking tray. Cover with the crumbs and place in a preheated oven at 180c/350f for 10 minutes until crumbs are brown.

Pour melted butter over the fish and return to the oven for 5 minutes.

Serve with the sauce and lemon wedges.

Sauce

Place the eggs in a pan of boiling water for 10 minutes.

Run the pan under cold water, remove the eggs and peel. Chop coarsely, using a round-bladed knife.

Melt the butter in a pan, add the flour and curry powder. Cook for 2 minutes, stirring all the time. Slowly add the milk, bring to the boil and simmer for 2 minutes.

Remove from the heat, add the coriander, eggs and seasoning, and stir well to combine.

47

Lemon Sole Goujons

with a Lime & Dill Sauce

ingredients
serves 6

900g/2lb Lemon sole,
skinned and filleted.

175g/6oz Fresh white
breadcrumbs. (Tip p.7)

2tbsp Seasoned flour.

2 Eggs, beaten.

575ml/1pt Sunflower oil.

Sauce

2 Egg yolks.

150ml/5floz Sunflower oil.

½tsp Dijon mustard.

1tbsp Chopped dill.

3 Limes, zest and juice.

method

Slice the fish into strips.

Dip into seasoned flour followed by the egg
and then the breadcrumbs.

Heat the oil in a pan until very hot. Fry the
fish until golden. Remove with a slotted
spoon and drain on kitchen paper. Keep
hot.

Sauce

Place the egg yolks in a mixing bowl. Add
the mustard, salt and pepper, whisk, add
1tsp very hot water, whisk.

Slowly add the oil followed by the lime juice
and rind. Add the dill. Serve with the fish.

Salmon Fillets

with Coconut & Lemon Grass

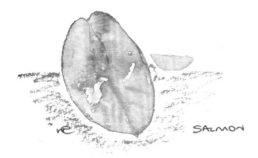

SALMON

TIP
When dealing with lemon grass you need to remove all the outer wraps that are tough. In most cases that is about ⅔ of the stalk. You will then find the tender aromatic stalk beneath.

ingredients
serves 6

1 Stalk Lemon grass, chopped.

220g/7oz Spinach, washed.

2.5cm/1" Root ginger, peeled and grated.

2 Cloves garlic, crushed.

6 Salmon fillets.

200ml/7floz Coconut milk.

2tsp Lime juice.

1tsp Golden caster sugar.

1dstsp Olive oil.

Salt and pepper.

method

Cook the spinach until wilted, drain and chop.

Heat the oil, add the ginger, garlic and Lemon Grass and soften. Add to spinach with salt and pepper.

Cut salmon in half vertically and sandwich with one sixth of the spinach mixture. Secure with cocktail sticks.

Place in a shallow dish.

Add the coconut milk, lime juice, sugar, salt and pepper and bake at 160c/325f for 20 minutes.

Smoked Haddock

& Egg Mousse

FLAT-LEAF PARSLEY

ingredients
serves 8

450g/1lb Smoked Haddock.

275ml/½pt Full fat milk.

2 Eggs, hard-boiled and chopped.

20g/¾oz Flour.

20g/¾oz Butter.

100ml/¼pt Mayonnaise, homemade (Tip p.90) or Hellman's Light.

1tbsp Chopped parsley.

15g/½oz Gelatine.

50ml/⅛pt Fish stock.

50ml/⅛pt Double cream, whipped.

Salt and pepper.

method

Poach fish in milk until it reaches simmering point. Remove from heat and cool. Reserve the milk.

Melt the butter in a pan and add the flour, cook for 2 minutes. Slowly add the poaching liquid and bring to the boil. Cook out for 2 minutes.

Flake the fish into a mixing bowl and remove all skin and bones.

Sprinkle gelatine onto cold stock and leave until spongy. Heat slowly to dissolve gelatine. Do not boil.

Add chopped eggs, parsley, mayonnaise and sauce to fish.

Add gelatine and whipped cream.

Season and chill.

Smoked Salmon & Dill Mousse

ingredients
serves 6

100g/4oz Smoked salmon.

100ml/¼pt Mayonnaise.
(Tip p.90)

100ml/¼pt Double cream,
lightly whipped.

100ml/¼pt Fish stock
(made with ½ a cube).

1tbsp Fresh dill, chopped.

6g/¼oz Powdered gelatine.

1 Lime, juiced.

Ground pepper.

method

Put the smoked salmon and lime juice in a food processor and whizz. Add the mayonnaise and dill and whiz again.

Sprinkle the gelatine over the fish stock and leave to go spongy.

Warm until the gelatine melts. Remove from the heat and cool. Do not let the gelatine boil otherwise it will go stringy when cold.

Add to the salmon mixture along with the cream and pepper.

Place in a bowl and chill. Serve with toast.

Smoked Salmon Rösti Cakes

with Tartare Sauce

ingredients
serves 6

450g Maris Piper potatoes, washed.

1tbsp Chives, snipped.

1 Egg yolk.

250g Smoked salmon, cut into strips.

110g Butter.

100ml Sunflower oil.

Salt and pepper.

Tartare Sauce

2 Egg yolks.

1tsp Dijon mustard.

1tbsp White wine vinegar.

200ml/7floz Sunflower oil.

10 Small gherkins, chopped.

1 heaped tsp Capers, chopped.

1dstsp Parsley, chopped.

Salt & pepper.

TIPS
When making mayonnaise, always use grease-free bowls and utensils. The hot water at the beginning will stop the sauce curdling. Do not use eggs from the fridge. They need to be at room temperature.

method

Place the potatoes in a saucepan and cover with cold water. Add salt. Bring to the boil and cook for 10 minutes. Drain. Cool slightly.

Peel and grate the potatoes. Add the rest of the ingredients and season well. Form into cakes. Pan fry for 5 minutes on each side in butter and oil.

Tartare Sauce

Whizz the egg yolks, salt, pepper, mustard and 1tbsp very hot water together for 2 minutes. Very slowly add some of the oil, then the vinegar and then the rest of the oil. If too thick add a little warm water.

Add the gherkins, capers and parsley and combine.

52

Scallops & Crayfish

en Croûte

ingredients
serves 6

225g/8oz Scallops.

175g/6oz Cooked crayfish.

275ml/½pt White wine,
reduced to 50ml/2floz.

150ml/¼pt Double cream.

150ml/¼pt Milk.

25g/1oz Butter.

25g/1oz Flour.

110g/4oz Grated Cheddar
cheese.

25g/1oz Grated Parmesan
cheese.

375g/10oz Ready-made all
butter puff pastry.

1 Egg yolk.

method

Roll out the pastry and cut into crescent shapes. Egg wash, cook in a hot oven until golden brown. Keep warm.

Place the scallops in a pan, pour over the milk. Heat gently until simmering point. Remove the fish from the liquid.

Melt the butter in a pan, add the flour and cook out for 2 minutes. Slowly add the milk, wine and cream, bring to the boil and cook out for 2 minutes.

Add the grated cheddar, stir until melted. Add the crayfish and scallops. Season.

Place the mixture in individual oven proof dishes. Sprinkle with Parmesan. Bake at 160c/325f for 15 minutes. Serve with the pastry shapes on the side of the dish.

Mussels in Thai Style Sauce

TIP

*Discard any mussels that do not open
when cooked. They are dead and will
make you ill.*

ingredients
serves 4

4tbsp Dry white wine.

Knob of butter.

1 Shallot, finely chopped.

450g/1lb Mussels in shell,
cleaned.

125ml/4½floz Low fat
coconut milk.

1 Fresh chilli, seeded and
finely chopped.

1tbsp Fresh chopped
coriander.

Salt and pepper.

method

Melt the butter and add the chilli and
shallots, and cook slowly for about 2
minutes, until soft but not coloured.

Add the wine and bring up to boiling point.

Add the mussels. Put the lid on the pan and
gently shake until the mussels open.

Remove the mussels from the pan with a
slotted spoon and keep warm.

Pour coconut milk into the pan and
heat until simmering point. Season, add
coriander and pour over the mussels.

Sri Lankan Prawns in Rice

ingredients
serves 8

275g/10oz Basmati rice, soaked for ½ hour in cold water.

1tsp Tomato paste.

450g/1lb Prawns in their shells, peeled. Reserve shells.

1 Level tsp Mild chilli powder.

2 Sticks of celery, chopped.

1 Medium onion, chopped.

2 Cloves of garlic, peeled and crushed.

1tbsp Olive oil.

1tsp Ginger, freshly grated.

1 Level tsp Cajun seasoning.

1tbsp Parsley, chopped.

575ml/1pt Prawn stock.

Stock

Shells from the prawns.

1 Onion, peeled and halved.

2 Sticks of celery, sliced.

1 Bay leaf.

6 Peppercorns.

1 Sprig of thyme.

½tsp Salt

Parsley stalks.

3pt Cold water.

method

Heat the oil in a pan, add the onion, garlic and celery, cook until golden brown.

Add the rice, tomato paste, chilli powder ginger and Cajun seasoning. Stir to combine all ingredients for 2 minutes.

Add the stock, bring to the boil, simmer for 12-15 minutes until the rice is cooked.

Add the prawns and heat through. Add the parsley. Serve.

Stock

Place everything in a large saucepan. Bring to the boil, simmer for 1 hour. Strain.

55

Chicken & Sesame Seed Goujons
with Spicy Tomato Dip

ingredients
serves 6

3 Chicken supremes.

15g/½oz Sesame seeds, dry toasted.

50g/2oz Flour mixed with salt and pepper.

2 Eggs beaten.

110g/4oz Fresh white breadcrumbs. (Tip p.7)

Dip

4 Large tomatoes, skinned seeded and chopped. (Tip p.32)

1 Onion, peeled and finely chopped.

1 Clove of garlic, peeled and crushed.

½tsp Chilli powder.

1dstsp Olive oil.

1tsp Chopped thyme.

Salt and Pepper.

method

Trim chicken and cut into small strips, approx 12-15 per breast.

Place strips in seasoned flour and shake off the excess.

Place in the beaten egg.

Mix the breadcrumbs with the sesame seeds and coat the chicken in them.

Deep fry the goujons in very hot sunflower oil. Drain on kitchen roll.

Serve with dip.

Dip

Place oil in a saucepan, add the onion and garlic cook until soft. Add the tomatoes, chilli salt and pepper and the thyme. Cook until soft.

Add a pinch of brown sugar.

Serve hot with the goujons.

Chicken

with Berries & Cherries

ingredients
serves 4-6

12 Chicken thighs, boned and skinned.

2 Cloves garlic, crushed.

12 Rashers thin, streaky, smoked bacon.

2tbsp Light soy sauce.

1tbsp Parsley, chopped.

340g Berries and cherries, dried, in vacuum packs.

Salt and Pepper.

method

Open up the chicken and remove any fat.

Add a little garlic, salt, pepper and a few berries. Close and wrap in bacon.

Place on a baking tray and sprinkle with the rest of the berries.

Pour over the soy sauce and sprinkle with parsley.

Cook in a hot oven at 160c/325f for 25-30 minutes until the bacon is crispy.

Ginger & Lime Chicken

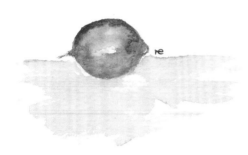

TIP

Always let meat come up to room temperature before cooking, as it will not then take fright and become tough and shrink, but will be moist and tender. If cooking a joint of meat always let it rest for at least 10 minutes before carving. This will make the meat firm up and make it easier to carve.

method

Slice the ginger and place in a glass bowl with the grated zest and juice of the limes, the honey, soy sauce and seasoning.

Place the chicken in the marinade and leave to stand in the refrigerator for a minimum of one hour.

ingredients

serves 6

6 Chicken breasts.

3 Limes, zest and juice.

50g/2oz Pickled ginger.

2tbsp Honey.

2tbsp Light soy sauce.

Remove the chicken from the juice and place in an ovenproof dish.

Let the chicken come back to room temperature. Place in a hot oven at 160c/325f for 20-25 minutes until the juices run clear.

Heat the marinade in a saucepan.

Pour this over the chicken when cooked.

Breast of Chicken

with a Mozzarella & Mustard Stuffing

method

Make a slit in the side of the chicken breast about 7.5cm/3" long.

ingredients
serves 6

6 Breasts of chicken.

250g/9oz Mozzarella, torn into 6 bits.

4tsp Grainy mustard.

12 Slices Parma ham.

6 Sage leaves.

Put a sixth of the mustard and mozzarella in the pocket.

Wrap in Parma ham. Top with a sage leaf. Roast 20-25 minutes at 180c/350f.

Remove from the pan and let the meat rest for 5 minutes.

Slice diagonally and place on a plate.

Serve.

Moroccan Pheasant

ingredients
serves 6

1tsp Fresh thyme, chopped.

1tbsp Sunflower oil.

3 Cloves garlic, crushed.

75g/3oz Ready to eat apricots, chopped.

1 Medium onion, chopped.

450g/1lb Minced pheasant, breast only.

1tsp Ground cinnamon.

2tsp Ground coriander.

3tbsp Worcestershire sauce.

400g/14oz Tin chopped tomatoes.

100ml/4floz Stock made with one chicken cube.

1tbsp Sun-dried tomato purée.

Salt and pepper.

50g/2oz Brown breadcrumbs.

50g/2oz Grated Gruyère cheese.

2tbsp chives, snipped.

300g/10oz Washed spinach.

15g/½oz Butter.

2tbsp Double cream.

¼ Nutmeg, grated.

method

Heat the oil in the pan, add the onion and garlic and soften. Add the mince and colour up. Add the apricots, cinnamon, coriander, thyme, Worcestershire sauce, chopped tomatoes, sun-dried tomato purée, stock and seasoning. Bring to the boil.

Cook at 170c/325f for approx 35 minutes.

Melt the butter in a saucepan and add the cream, nutmeg and seasoning. Add the spinach and wilt. Place in an ovenproof dish.

Pour the meat sauce over the top.

Mix the breadcrumbs, cheese and chives together and cover the top of the meat.

Bake until golden brown at 170c/325f.

Duck Breasts

with Blackberry Sauce

method

Score the fat on the duck. Rub the allspice and seasoning over the breast.

Pour the red wine, Crème de Mure, cinnamon, star anise and grated rind of the orange into a pan. Bring to the boil.

ingredients
serves 4

Cook the duck, skin side down, in a dry pan, for 4-5 minutes until golden brown. Turn the meat over and cook for a further 6 minutes.

4 Duck breasts.

1 Pinch Allspice.

Take off the heat, remove the fat and leave to stand for 10 minutes.

5tbsp Crème de Mure.

5tbsp Red wine.

Add half the orange juice to the sauce, simmer for 5 minutes.

½ Small cinnamon stick.

1 Star anise.

Blend the rest of the orange juice with the cornflour. Add to the sauce, stirring all the time.

1 Orange, juice and rind of.

300g/10½oz Blackberries.

Heat the blackberries gently in the sauce. Add the meat juices to the sauce.

2 level tsp Cornflour.

Slice the duck and serve with the sauce.

Pheasant

with Port, Celery & Chestnuts

REDCURRANT

ingredients
serves 6-8

110g/4oz Red currant jelly.

100ml/¼pt Port.

2 Pheasants.

200g/7oz Vacuum packed
Chestnuts.

4 Sticks celery.

1 Onion.

1 Bay leaf.

Small sprig of thyme.

55g/2oz Butter.

55g/2oz Flour.

Salt and pepper.

method

Put the pheasants in a pot and cover with
cold water.

Add 2 sticks of the celery, roughly chopped
onion and skin, bay leaf, thyme, salt and
pepper.

Bring to the boil, reduce the heat to
simmering point. Poach for approximately 1
hour until tender (test with a carving fork).

Take the birds out of the cooking liquor and
cool. Strain the pheasant stock through a
fine sieve.

Melt the butter in a pan, add the flour and
cook for 2 minutes, stirring all the time to
get rid of the raw taste of flour.

Add the port and red currant jelly. Slowly
add some of the stock, to make a coating
sauce. Add the rest of the celery and the
chestnuts. Adjust the seasoning. Simmer
for 10 minutes.

Take the pheasant meat off the bone. Add
the meat to the sauce. Cool.

To reheat cook for approximately ½ hour at
160c/300f.

Guinea Fowl with Madeira
& Spiced Satsumas

ingredients
serves 4

1 tbsp Oil.

25g/1oz Butter.

8 Guinea Fowl joints.

225g/8oz Shallots.

225g/8oz Streaky bacon, cut into strips.

6 Satsumas, quartered.

1 Orange, juiced.

2½cm/1" Piece root ginger, peeled and grated.

2 Cloves garlic, crushed.

2 level tbsp Plain flour.

275ml/½pt Madeira.

575ml/1pt Chicken stock made with 2 cubes.

1 Cinnamon stick.

3 level tbsp Red currant jelly.

1 Sprig thyme.

1 Bay leaf.

method

Heat the oil in a large casserole dish and brown the Guinea Fowl on all sides. Remove.

Put the shallots and bacon in the pan and brown. Add the satsumas and brown.

Add the garlic, ginger and flour, and cook out.

Add the Madeira and stock, and bring to the simmer.

Add the thyme, bay leaf, orange juice, cinnamon and red currant jelly.

Add the Guinea Fowl and cook for approx 1½ hours at 160c/300f until tender.

Remove the cinnamon stick. Take out the Guinea Fowl and keep warm.

Reduce the cooking liquor until syrupy. Pour over the birds and serve.

63

Venison Cobbler

ingredients
serves 6-8

1kg/2lb Diced venison.

2 Carrots, peeled and chopped.

1 Medium onion, peeled and chopped.

2 Sticks celery, chopped.

1 Bay leaf.

1tbsp Red currant jelly.

100ml/¼pt Port.

75g/3oz Butter.

40g/1½oz Flour.

850ml/1½pt Beef stock made with 2 cubes.

The Cobbler

225g/8oz Self-raising flour.

½tsp Salt.

50g/2oz Butter.

100ml/¼pt Milk.

1tsp Parsley, chopped.

1 Egg yolk.

method

Melt half the butter in a casserole dish. Add the meat and brown all over. Remove.

Melt the rest of the butter. Add the onion, carrot and celery and brown. Add the flour and cook out for 2 minutes.

Add the port, red currant jelly and then slowly add the stock, stirring all the time. Bring to the boil and add the bay leaf. Simmer for 2 minutes.

Place in the oven at 170c/325f for approx 1½ hours until tender.

The Cobbler

Rub the flour, salt and butter together until it resembles fine breadcrumbs. Add milk and parsley with a knife. Roll out and cut into rounds. Glaze with egg yolk.

Place the cobbler on top of the meat and bake at 200c/400f for approx 20 minutes until golden brown and risen.

Fillet of Beef en Croûte

with Mushroom Duxelles

ingredients
serves 6

1kg/2lb Fillet of beef, trimmed.

375g/10oz Packet of all butter puff pastry.

1tbsp Olive oil.

1 Egg yolk.

275g/10oz Chestnut mushrooms, finely chopped.

75g/3oz Fresh white breadcrumbs. (Tip p.7)

1tsp Parsley, chopped.

1tsp Thyme, chopped.

1 Small onion, finely chopped.

1 Clove of garlic, crushed.

50g/2oz butter.

Béarnaise Sauce.

method

Cut one third off the pastry, leaving two thirds. Roll out the smaller piece on a floured surface to the same size as the beef. Trim the edges, place on a baking tray. Prick the pastry all over, then bake for about 20-25 minutes at 180c/350f until golden brown. Cool.

Fry the beef in a pan in the olive oil until browned all over. Remove from the pan.

To make the duxelles stuffing, melt the butter in a saucepan add the onion and garlic, and cook until soft but not coloured. Add the mushrooms and cook for a further 5 minutes. Add the breadcrumbs, herbs and salt and pepper. Cool.

Roll out the remaining pastry to 7.5cm/3"larger all around, than the cooked pastry. Trim the edges, then wet with cold water. Place the beef on the cooked pastry, add the duxelles over the top and sides.

Place the uncooked pastry centrally over the top. Wrap underneath and make a firm join. Egg wash. Bake at 180c/350f for about 25 minutes until the pastry is golden brown. Remove from the oven and let the meat rest for at least 5 minutes before carving.

Serve with Béarnaise sauce (See p.66)

Béarnaise Sauce

TIPS

If you find that Béarnaise (or Hollandaise) sauce curdles, add an ice cube and whisk hard. If it doesn't work with the first one, try again. It will work.

Always use bowls and utensils that are completely free of grease.

Always keep your sauce warm, not hot. ie. just above room temperature. I keep mine over a bowl of hot water until needed.

Do not put the sauce in a refrigerator as it will set hard.

ingredients
makes enough for 6-8

3 Egg yolks.

225g/8oz butter, melted.

2tsp Parsley, chopped.

2tsp Tarragon, chopped.

200ml/7floz White wine vinegar.

1 Shallot, peeled and sliced.

Ground black pepper.

The stalks from the herbs.

1 Bay leaf.

method

Place the vinegar, shallot, pepper, herb stalks and bay leaf in a saucepan and boil to reduce, until there is only a tablespoon of fluid left in the pan.

Pass through a sieve.

Place the egg yolks in a bowl over hot water, whisking all the time with a hand whisk, until pale and creamy in colour. Add the reduction. Slowly add the melted butter, followed by the herbs. Pour into a warm sauce boat and serve with the beef.

Lamb Hot Pot

TURNIP

ingredients
serves 8

6 Neck fillets of lamb, sliced.

110g/4oz Butter.

50g/2oz Flour.

1500ml/2½pt Chicken stock made with 2 stock cubes.

2 Parsnips, peeled and diced.

4 Small turnips, peeled and diced.

4 Medium carrots, peeled and diced.

½ Small swede, peeled and diced.

1 Sprig thyme.

1 Bay leaf.

1kg/2lb Old potatoes, peeled and sliced.

method

Melt 25g/1oz butter in a casserole dish. Add the meat and brown all over. Remove.

Melt 50g/2oz butter in the pan and add all the vegetables and fry until slightly brown. Add flour and cook out for 2 minutes. Slowly add stock, stirring all the time, and bring to the boil.

Add meat, thyme and bay leaf.

Place in a shallow ovenproof dish and arrange the potatoes on top with remaining butter dotted over the potato.

Cook for approx 1½-2 hours until the meat is tender and potatoes cooked.

Best End of Lamb with a

Red Currant & Balsamic Sauce

ingredients
serves 4

2 Best ends of lamb, French trimmed.

110g/4oz Fresh white breadcrumbs. (Tip p.7)

2tbs Chopped fresh mint.

1tbs Sesame seeds.

1tbs Dijon mustard.

1 Egg yolk.

Salt and pepper.

Sauce

25g/1oz Butter.

25g/1oz Flour.

575ml/1pt Beef stock.

2tsp Soy sauce.

2tbs Balsamic vinegar.

2tbs Red currant jelly.

1 Onion, peeled and sliced.

method

Mix the breadcrumbs, mint, seeds, mustard, egg yolk and seasoning together in a bowl. Press the mixture together.

Place half the mixture on each rack on the non-bone side.

Roast in an oven at 180c/350f for 15-20 minutes. Rest for 10 minutes. Carve and serve with sauce.

Sauce

Melt the butter in a pan, add the onion and cook until brown. Add the flour and cook out for 2 minutes. Slowly add the stock, soy sauce, vinegar and jelly. Simmer for 5 minutes. Check seasoning and serve with the lamb.

Braised Sausages with Lentils & Peppadew Peppers

ingredients
serves 6

450g/1lb Pork sausages.

1tbsp Olive oil.

2 Red onions, sliced.

10 Peppadews, sliced.

1tsp Cumin.

150ml/5floz Chicken stock made with ½ a stock cube.

575ml/1pt Red wine, reduced to 200ml/7floz.

420g/15oz Tin of cooked lentils, drained and rinsed.

½tsp Fresh thyme, chopped.

1tsp Parsley, chopped.

method

Pour the oil into a casserole dish, add the sausages and brown all over. Add the onions, brown.

Add the peppadews and cumin. Cook for 2 minutes.

Add the red wine and stock. Season.

Bring to the boil. Add the lentils and thyme.

Place in an oven at 160c/325f and cook for approx 30 minutes, until most of the liquid has been absorbed.

Garnish with the chopped parsley.

Serve.

Andalusian Pork

GARLIC

ingredients
serves 6

1kg/2lb Pork tenderloin, trimmed.

2tbsp Paprika.

1tsp Oregano, chopped.

1tsp Thyme, chopped.

1 Clove of garlic, crushed.

2tbsp Olive oil.

Salt and pepper.

Sauce

½pt Double cream.

1tsp Oregano, chopped.

Grated rind of 1 lemon.

1tsp Paprika.

method

Mix the paprika, herbs, garlic, oil and seasoning. Spread over the meat. Leave to marinade for a minimum of 1 hour in a refrigerator.

Let the meat come back to room temperature. Place on a baking tray and roast in a hot oven at 180c/350f for 15 minutes.

Remove from the tray and place on a plate. Let it rest before carving.

Carve the meat and serve the sauce on the side.

Sauce

Pour the juices from the pan into a saucepan, add the cream, oregano, lemon rind and paprika, bring to the boil and let it thicken slightly. Adjust the seasoning.

For a less rich sauce, use half fat crème fraîche instead of the cream.

Pork Tenderloin

Stuffed with Prunes & Pistachio Nuts

ingredients
serves 6

2 Pork fillets, trimmed.

1 Onion, peeled and chopped.

1 Cooking apple, peeled and chopped.

25g/1oz Butter.

25g/1oz Pistachio nuts, roughly chopped.

1tsp Chopped sage.

110g/4oz Fresh white breadcrumbs. (Tip p.7)

1 Egg yolk.

110g/4oz Prunes, roughly chopped.

8 Slices Parma ham.

Sauce

3tbs Calvados.

275/½pt Double cream.

1tbsp Grainy mustard.

Salt and pepper.

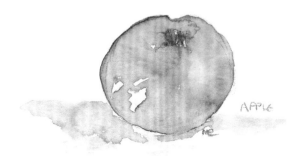
APPLE

method

Melt the butter in a pan and add the onion and apple. Cook until soft.

Add the prunes, egg yolk, nuts, sage, breadcrumbs, salt and pepper. Mix together to bind. If too dry add a little milk.

Cut the pork fillets halfway through, lengthways. Open them up and place the stuffing in the cavity. Then wrap the fillet up in Parma ham. Each fillet needs four slices.

Place in a hot oven at 180c/350f for 20 minutes.

Remove and let the meat rest for 10 minutes.

Sauce

Heat the Calvados in a pan to reduce slightly. Add the double cream and grainy mustard. Boil.

Slice the meat. Serve the sauce separately.

Pork Tenderloin

with Orange Sauce

ingredients
serves 6

2 Pork tenderloins, trimmed.

25g/1oz Butter.

2tsp Fresh rosemary, chopped.

Sauce

1 Onion, chopped.

25g/1oz Butter.

25g/1oz Flour.

575ml/1pt Chicken stock.

2 Oranges.

2tbsp Caster sugar.

1tbsp White wine vinegar.

50ml/2floz Port.

method

Sauce

Melt the butter in a pan, add the onion and cook until golden brown. Add the flour and cook out. Slowly add the stock, bring to the boil and simmer 10 minutes. Strain.

Peel the oranges with a potato peeler. Cut into thin strips and blanch in boiling water for 3 minutes. Cut the pith from the orange, cut out the segments and place in a dish.

Place the sugar in a pan, cover with cold water, bring to the boil and cook until the sugar turns to caramel. Take off the heat. Add the vinegar and port. Add the orange rind to the sauce.

Pork

Melt the butter, add the pork, season and add the rosemary. Brown the meat all over. Place in an oven at 160c/325f and cook for 15-20 minutes. Remove from the oven and let the meat relax for 15 minutes.

Spicy Pork Belly
with Crispy Crackling

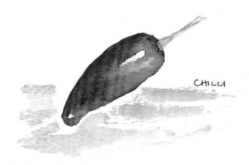

CHILLI

ingredients
serves 8

Handful of fresh Bay leaves.

2tsp Rock salt.

1tbsp Paprika.

3tsp Ground cumin.

1tsp Ground coriander.

1tsp Ground black pepper.

1tbsp Oil.

2kg/5lb Pork belly, skin removed (to be cooked separately).

2 Red chillies, seeded and chopped.

1tbsp Coriander, chopped.

1tbsp Olive oil.

method

Bash the bay leaves and salt in a pestle and mortar until leaves disintegrate and salt turns green. Discard any strands.

Add the rest of the spices.

Rub the spice mix and oil onto the pork. Place in a roasting tin and cover with foil, non-shiny side next to the pork.

Roast for approx 2 hours at 160c/325f. Remove from the oven and let the meat rest for 15 minutes.

Place the skin on a cooling wire on a baking tray and cook at 180c/350f until crisp.

Mix chillies, coriander and olive oil together and pour mix over the top. Slice and serve with the crispy skin cut into 8 pieces.

Blackberry Mousse
topped with Coulis

method

Cook blackberries with the sugar until the juice runs. Cool, then whizz in processor and sieve.

Whisk egg yolks and sugar until ribbon stage and add two thirds of fruit puree.

Soak gelatine in the lemon juice until spongy. Melt over low heat until gelatine has melted.

Add gelatine to the egg yolks and fruit purée.

Whip double cream and add to mixture.

Chill until starting to set.

Whip egg whites until peaks form. Fold into mixture.

Chill until set.

Pour rest of the puree over the top.

ingredients
serves 8

1kg/2lb Wild blackberries.

100gm/4oz Caster sugar.

5 Eggs, separated.

25g/1oz Powdered gelatine.

300ml/½pt Double cream.

100gm/4oz Caster sugar.

Blueberry & Yoghurt Pots

ingredients
serves 8

300g/10oz Blueberries.

1tbsp Caster sugar.

1 Orange, grated zest.

½ Orange, juiced.

450g/1lb Blueberry yoghurt.

200g/7oz Fromage frais.

Custard

150ml/5floz Milk.

1 Egg yolk.

1tsp Vanilla essence.

1tsp Cornflour.

1tbsp Caster sugar.

150ml/5floz Double cream.

method

Custard

Heat the milk, cream and vanilla essence until simmering.

Whisk egg yolk, cornflour and caster sugar together until pale and creamy. Pour milk mixture onto the egg mixture, stirring all the time. Return to the pan and bring to the boil. Simmer for 2 minutes and then cool.

Compote

Place blueberries and sugar in a pan with the juice and rind of the orange. Bring to the boil and simmer for 3-4 minutes. Cool.

Place the compote in the bottom of a serving dish.

Combine yoghurt, cooled custard and fromage frais together and spoon over the compote.

Serve with a sprig of mint on the top.

Lemon & Ginger Syllabub

ingredients

serves 8

200g/7oz Caster sugar.

200ml/7floz Dry sherry.

1 Lemon, grated rind and juice.

575ml/1pt Double cream.

2tsp Stem ginger, finely chopped.

method

Put the sugar, sherry and lemon juice in a bowl and stir.

Lightly whip the cream with the grated lemon rind until soft peak stage.

Fold the sherry mixture and the stem ginger into the cream.

Place in individual glasses. Chill before serving.

Fruit Brûlée

method

Place fruit in a saucepan with the caster sugar and heat for approx 5 minutes until sugar melts and juices run. Place fruit in a flan dish with a little of the juice and cool, with a little of the juice

Whip the double cream until the same consistency as the yoghurt. Mix the two together. Place on top of the chilled fruit mixture and chill.

Approx 2 hours before serving, cover with brown sugar and grill.

ingredients
serves 6-8

Chill until ready to serve.

700g/1½lb Mixed red fruits.

110g/4oz Caster sugar.

225g/8oz Greek yoghurt.

225g/8oz Double cream.

175g/6oz Demerara sugar.

You can also make this with peaches or nectarines that you skin first then toss in freshly squeezed orange juice, to stop them discolouring.

To peel the fruit, make a small incision with a knife in the top of the fruit, drop into a pan of boiling water for 10 seconds, remove from the water and peel.

Chocolate & Cardamom Pots

method

Pour the cream, cardamom, vanilla and rum into a pan. Heat to just below boiling point. Remove from the heat and leave to stand for 15 minutes.

Place the chocolate in a bowl.

Reheat the cream mixture. Pour through a sieve onto the chocolate. Stir until it is melted. Pour into glasses and chill.

Let the chocolate mixture come to room temperature before serving.

Decorate with crème fraîche and coffee beans.

If you don't like cardamom add another tsp of vanilla extract instead.

ingredients
serves 8-10

400ml/14floz Single cream.

3 Cardamom pods crushed.

1tsp Vanilla extract.

1tbsp Rum.

125g/4½oz Dark chocolate, chopped.

4tbsp Crème fraîche.

Chocolate covered coffee beans to decorate.

Lemon Curd Syllabub

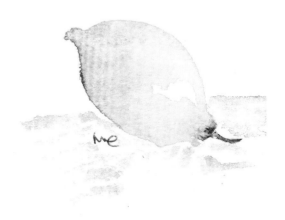

ingredients
serves 8

110g/4oz Unsalted butter, melted.

3 Eggs.

3 Egg yolks.

225g/8oz Caster sugar.

3 Lemons, rinded.

100ml/4floz Lemon juice.

300ml/10½floz Double cream.

250g/9oz Meringues, broken up.

method

Whisk the eggs, egg yolks, caster sugar, lemon rind and juice until pale and creamy.

Add the hot melted butter.

Cook in microwave for 2 minutes. Take out and whisk. Put back in microwave and repeat until thick. Cool.

Whisk the double cream until soft peaks. Fold in the broken meringues.

Spoon some lemon curd into a serving dish followed by the cream and meringue and continue layering.

Serve chilled.

Plum & Custard, Crumble Tart

ingredients
serves 8-10

Pastry

325g/12oz Plain flour

225g/8oz Diced butter

Grated rind of 1 orange

75g/3oz Ground almonds.

75g/3oz Caster sugar.

2 Egg yolks.

2 tbsp Cold water.

Crumble

170g/6oz Flour

110g/4oz Diced butter.

50g/2oz Light Muscovado sugar

Pinch of salt.

Filling

2 Eggs

2 Egg yolks.

2 Oranges, grated rind and juice.

1tbsp Cornflour.

275ml/10floz Double cream.

2 Star anise.

150g/5oz Caster sugar.

450g/1lb Plums halved and stoned.

method

Pastry
Place the flour, orange rind, almonds and butter in a food processor and whizz until it resembles fine breadcrumbs. Add the sugar and whizz. Add the water and egg yolks, whizz again until the mixture balls up.

Wrap in cling film and chill for 30 minutes. Roll out, line a greased flan dish. Cook blind.

Crumble
Place the flour, salt and butter in a bowl and rub in until it resembles coarse breadcrumbs. Add the sugar.

Place on a baking tray. Bake at 160c/325f for 12-15 minutes until golden brown. Keep warm.

Filling
Place the plums in an ovenproof bowl, add half the sugar, star anise and the orange juice. Cover with foil. Bake at 160c/325f until soft – approx 30 minutes. Cool.

Whisk the remaining sugar, cornflour, eggs, egg yolks and orange rind together until pale and creamy. Pour the cream into a pan, bring to simmering point and pour over the egg mixture, whisking all the time. Return to the pan and cook out for 2 minutes.

Place the drained plums in the pastry case, add the custard. Bake at 160c/325f until set - about 15 minutes.

Scatter the crumble mixture over the top. Serve warm.

Mango & Passion Fruit Roulade

method

Beat the egg whites until stiff but not dry. Slowly add the sugar until thick and shiny. Add the cornflour, vinegar and vanilla.

Place the mixture in a baking tray that has been lined with non-stick baking paper.

Level the surface. Bake at 160c/300f for about 30 minutes until the surface is firm.

Cover the surface of the roulade with a damp tea towel until cool.
Turn out onto a sheet of non-stick baking paper, which has been dusted with icing sugar.

Spread the yogurt over the roulade, followed by the passion fruit and mango.

Roll up. Sprinkle with a little more icing sugar.

Chill for at least 1 hour. Slice and serve.

ingredients
serves 6-8

3 Large egg whites.

175g/6oz Caster sugar.

1 level tsp Cornflour.

1tsp White wine vinegar.

1tsp Vanilla extract.

200g/7oz Fat-free Greek yogurt.

1 Mango, peeled and sliced.

4 Passion fruit, halved and seeds removed.

Icing sugar to dust.

Ginger & Rhubarb Trifle

ingredients
serves 10

20 Ginger snap biscuits, crushed.

275ml/10floz Double cream, whipped to soft peak stage.

900g/2lb Rhubarb, chopped up.

1 Orange, rind and juice.

300g/10½oz Sponge cakes, sliced.

110g/4oz Caster sugar.

50ml/2floz Ginger wine.

6 Pieces of stem ginger, chopped.

Custard

4 Egg yolks.

1tsp Cornflour.

425ml/15floz Double cream.

25g/1oz Caster sugar.

1tsp Vanilla extract. (Tip p.90)

RHUBARB.

method

Whisk the egg yolks, vanilla, sugar and cornflour together. Heat the cream to simmering point and pour onto the egg mixture, stirring all the time. Return to the saucepan and cook out. Cool.

Place the rhubarb in an ovenproof dish, sprinkle with sugar, pour over the orange juice and rind. Cover with foil. Bake at 160c/325f until the rhubarb is soft. Cool.

Place one third of the sponge in a glass bowl, sprinkle over half the ginger wine, half the rhubarb, half the ginger snaps and chopped stem ginger. Repeat, ending with the cake on top.

Pour the custard over the cake, followed by the cream. Sprinkle the remainder of the brandy snaps over the top just before serving.

Rhubarb & Ginger

Custard Pudding

TIP
A water bath is a roasting tin, one third filled with hot water. It is used to stop the dish separating.

ingredients
serves 6-8

325g/12oz Madeira cake, slightly stale.

325g/12oz Trimmed rhubarb in 1cm/½" lengths.

75g/3oz Golden caster sugar.

100g/4oz Stem ginger, sliced.

Custard

275ml/½pt Milk.

575ml/1pt Double cream.

3 Whole eggs.

3 Egg yolks.

2tbsp Cornflour.

2tbsp Caster sugar.

1tsp Vanilla extract. (Tip p.90)

method

Grease a 2ltr/3½pt ovenproof dish.

Slice the cake and lie it in the bottom of the dish. Sprinkle the rhubarb and ginger over the top followed by the golden caster sugar.

Put the milk and cream in a heavy based pan with the vanilla essence and heat.

Whisk the eggs, sugar and yolks together until thick. Add the cornflour and whisk again.

Bring the cream and milk to the boil. Slowly pour over the egg mixture, whisking all the time.

Pour the custard over the sponge and rhubarb.

Place the dish in a water bath. Bake for 45-50 minutes at 190c/375f until set and golden.

Frozen Chocolate & Orange

Cheesecake

TIP
To melt the chocolate, break into small
pieces and place in a bowl over a pan
of hot water. Do not let the water
touch the bowl, or let the water boil,
as this will result in the chocolate over
heating. It will split and you can't do
anything with it.

ingredients
serves 10

225g/8oz Crushed digestive
biscuits.

75g/3oz Melted butter.

225g/8oz Full fat cream
cheese.

1tsp Vanilla extract.

100g/4oz Caster sugar.

175g/6oz Dark chocolate,
melted.

2 Oranges, zest.

2 Eggs, beaten.

2 Egg whites.

125ml/¼pt Double cream,
whipped to soft peak stage.

method

Mix the biscuits and butter together and
place in a 25cm/10" spring-loaded tin
lined with non-stick paper and bake for 10
minutes at 180c/350f.

Beat the cream cheese, vanilla extract and
half the sugar together. Add the cooled
chocolate, zest of the two oranges, two
eggs and the cream to the mixture.

Beat the egg whites to the soft peak stage
and slowly add the second half of the sugar
and whisk until thick and glossy.

Fold into creamy mixture and pour over the
base.

Freeze and then remove from the freezer
30 minutes before eating and place in the
fridge.

Passion Fruit & Apricot

Ice Cream Cake

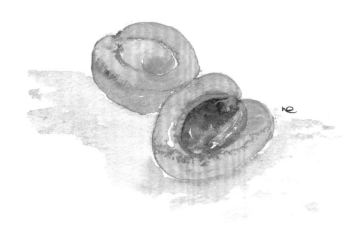

ingredients
serves 12

425ml/15floz Double cream, whipped to soft peak stage.

450g/1lb Apricot yoghurt.

175g/6oz Sifted icing sugar.

4 Lemons, zest.

150g/5oz Crushed meringues.

7tbsp Lemon curd.

2 Passion fruit.

method

Mix the cream, yogurt, icing sugar and grated lemon rind together.

Fold in the lemon curd, meringues and the pulp from the passion fruit.

Pour the mixture into a greased foil lined cake tin, preferably spring loaded.

Cover the top of the tin with cling film, place in a freezer bag.

Freeze for at least 24 hours.

Remove from the freezer just before serving.

You could dust a little cinnamon over the top.

Cinnamon Pears

ingredients

serves 6

6 Large pears, not too ripe.

2tbsp Honey.

1tsp Ground cinnamon.

1 Cinnamon stick.

150ml/¼pt Water.

method

Peel and core the pears, leaving the stalks on.

Place in a baking dish. Pour over the honey.

Sprinkle the cinnamon over the top, add the cinnamon stick and the water.

Place the dish in an oven at 160c/325f for about 45 minutes to 1 hour until soft, turning the fruit around once or twice during cooking.

Serve hot or cold with cream or crème fraîche.

Mini Lemon Tarts

TIP

To bake blind small pastry shells, place an identical tin over the top of the pastry shells, press down lightly and cook until the sides of the pastry are dry enough not to collapse. Remove the top tin and carry on baking until golden brown.

ingredients
makes 36 small or 1 large

Pastry

225g/8oz Plain flour.

110g/4oz Butter, diced.

50g/2oz Caster sugar.

¾tbsp Cold water.

Filling

150ml/¼pt Double cream.

4 Eggs.

1 Egg yolk.

2 lemons, juiced.

90g/3½oz Caster sugar.

90g/3½oz Butter.

method

Pastry

Place all dry ingredients in a food processor with a plastic blade. Whizz until it resembles fine breadcrumbs. Add the water slowly until the mixture starts to come together.

Turn out onto a floured surface and roll out. Cut into circles to fit a small muffin tin. Place circles into greased tin and prick the bottom of the pastry with a fork. Bake at 160c/325f for approx 15 minutes until golden brown.

Filling

Whisk together the eggs, egg yolk, lemon juice and sugar. Heat the butter until melted and add to the egg mixture. Place the bowl over hot water and whisk occasionally until thickened. Then add the cream. Place filling in pastry shells, and bake for about 10 minutes at 160c/325f until set but not too firm.

Moist Plum & Orange Cake

ingredients
serves 6-8

450g/1lb Plums, stoned and halved.

1 Orange, grated rind and juice.

50g/2oz Golden caster sugar.

½ a vanilla pod, split.

Cake

150g/5oz Butter.

150g/5oz Golden caster sugar.

2 Large eggs, beaten.

90g/3½oz Self raising flour.

110g/4oz Ground almonds.

½tsp Baking powder.

Topping

1 Orange, zest.

25g/1oz Butter.

25g/1oz Soft brown sugar.

50g/2oz Flaked almonds.

method

Place the plums in an ovenproof dish, add the sugar, orange rind and juice and the seeds from the vanilla pod, plus the pod.

Cover with tin foil, bake at 180c/350f for approx 30 minutes, until the fruit is soft. Cool. Remove the vanilla pod.

Cake

Beat the sugar and butter together until light and fluffy.

Slowly add the eggs. Fold in the flour, baking powder and almonds.
Place in a spring-loaded tin, lined with non-stick baking paper.

Push the plums and juice into and over the cake. Bake for 30 minutes at 180c/350f.

Topping

Melt the butter in a pan, stir in the sugar, almonds and orange rind.
Dot the mixture over the half cooked cake.

Return the cake to the oven for a further 30 minutes, until firm to the touch.

Cool. This will freeze.

Extra Hints & Tips

1. Any vegetable that grows below the soil, cook in cold water, with the exception of new potatoes which should be cooked in boiling water.

2. All vegetables that grow above the soil, cook in water that is already boiling.

3. Always put salt into the pan of green vegetables at the end of the cooking time. Salt slows down the cooking process.

4. Always defrost prawns in the refrigerator. They have a very delicate flavour and should never be defrosted in water, as what little flavour they have will disappear.

5. To clean chicken livers, remove all green bits. This is the bile and will make your pâté bitter if not removed. Also remove any sinews you find.

6. Don't wash mushrooms, as they will go slimy. Wipe them with kitchen roll instead.

7. Don't store eggs in the refrigerator. They must be room temperature before use.

8. When making pastry in a food processor, always use the plastic blade. The end result will be much better.

9. When cooking meat, after you remove it from the oven, keep it warm and let it rest for at least 10 minutes. This will make carving much easier.

10. The skin on peppers is very indigestible. To remove it, place the peppers on a baking tray and put into a hot oven until the skin is charred. Remove from the oven, place a clean tea towel over the top and leave to cool. Peel the skin off and remove the seed.

11. When peeling and coring apples, place them in a bowl with water and lemon juice to stop discolouration.

12. When making mayonnaise, always add a drop of very hot water, at the beginning with the egg and seasonings. Then whisk well before adding the oil. This will help to stop it splitting.

13. When you make meringues, or mayonnaise, always make sure that your bowl and whisk are completely free of grease. If in any doubt wash again, in plenty of hot soapy water.

14. If you use dried herbs instead of fresh, use only half the quantity. They are much stronger but the flavour is not as good.

15. If you are making a beef or fish en croûte, cook the pastry base first. This will ensure that the pastry remains crisp.

16. Double cream that is very fresh will take a long time to whip. Cream that is taken straight out of the refrigerator will also take a long time to whip, but cream at room temperature will whip very quickly.

17. Don't buy vanilla or almond essence as they have very little flavour. Buy extracts, these are a lot more expensive, but are very concentrated, so that you only need a small amount.

18. Fry nuts in sunflower oil, before adding to a salad. They will then become crisp and have a much more pronounced flavour. Fry until golden and drain on kitchen roll. If you sieve the oil after use, it makes an excellent base for a salad dressing.

Index

Index

Index

Index

Index